Written by Roderick Hunt
Illustrated by Alex Brychta

Get on.

D1080438

3

Get on, Biff.

Biff got on.

5

Get on, Chip.

Chip got on.

Get on, Kipper.

Kipper got on.

Oh, no!

Talk about the story

Maze

Help Biff and Chip get to the sea.

Who Can You See?

Written by Roderick Hunt
Illustrated by Alex Brychta

Who can you see?

Biff…

…and Chip.

Mum…

...and Kipper.

Floppy…

...and a spaceman.

No. It is Dad!

Talk about the story

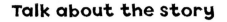

Where was the family?

What shape did Chip make with his hands?

What was Dad wearing?

Which shapes can you make with your shadow?

Match the shadows

Can you match the shadows to the characters?